VOCABIRDS

VOCABULARY WORKBOOK

GRADE 2

OM KIDZ
An Imprint of Om Books International

WHO AM I?

Help the Vocabird to learn new words by matching the pictures to the correct words.

fireman

baby

tailor

animals

dolphin

cherry

beehive

SPELL CHECK

Unscramble the letters and fill in the blanks with the names of the pictures given below.

cihckne

chicken

sepgra

____

sehroeas

____

eykhoc

____

erlfow

____

dcotor

____

Picture Perfect

Look at the pictures. Spell their names and complete the crossword on the next page for the Vocabirds.

Across

1) 

2) 

3) 

4) 

Down

5) 

6) 

7) 

8) 

Picture Perfect

CONSO-HUNT

Look at the pictures and fill in the blanks with the correct consonants.

1) 

2) 

3) 

4) 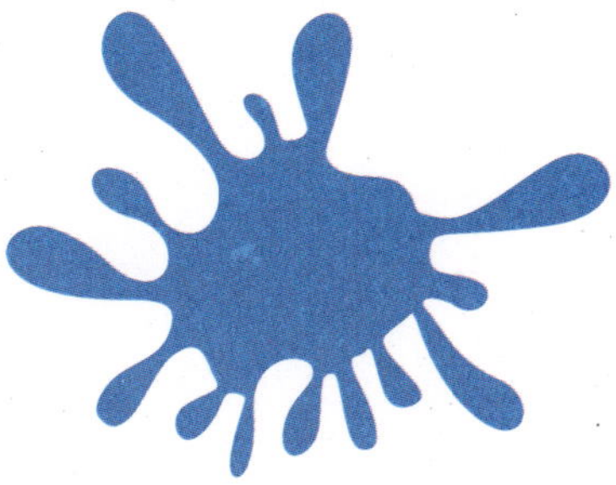

5) 

6) 

1) _c_ _r_ a _b_

2) ___ ___ a ___ e ___

3) ___ ___ ee

4) ___ ___ ue

5) ___ ___ ee ___

6) ___ ___ u ___

Blended Codes

Colour the petals according to the consonant blends written on them. The colour code is given below.

Voca tip: A consonant blend is a mix of consonant sounds in a word. For example: "pl" in play.

pl sn br tr cl

pluck	bridge	clumsy	plum
snail	clue	train	cluster
broom	sneak	brim	plaster
snow	trim	brand	trumpet

FUN WITH DIGRAPHS

Look at the pictures. Tick the picture whose name has a consonant digraph.

Voca tip: When two consonants create one sound in a word, we call it a digraph. For example, ch, sh, th and wh.

wheat ✓

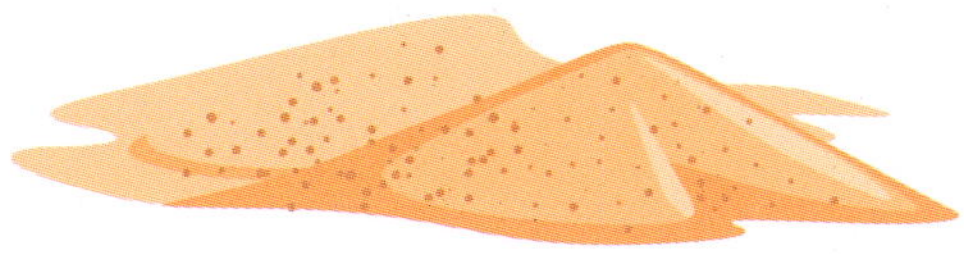

sand ◯

beach ◯

cloud ◯

dolphin ◯

water ◯

octopus ◯

shark ◯

EUREKA!

Make new words from the digraphs and blends given in the centre.

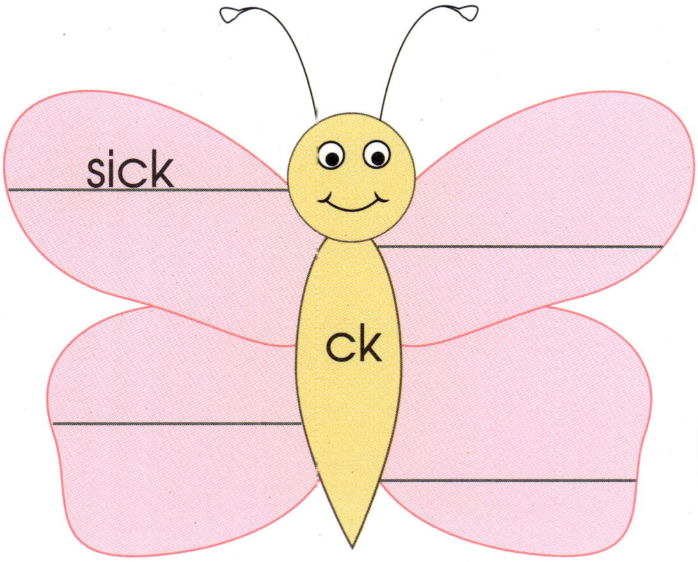

RHYME TIME

Read the first word and circle its rhyming word in each row.

Voca tip: Rhyming words have similar sounds.

bear	sit	ship	care	but
red	bed	tile	tear	touch
tough	teach	seek	big	rough
right	bat	left	might	small
late	kit	gate	fight	rail
blue	true	skit	tick	car
niece	stand	run	which	peace
check	cold	blue	deck	tan
know	grow	wet	bye	ring

RHYMTASTIC

Read the poem carefully and list the rhyming words in it.

The Squirrel

Teeny, tiny
Hippity hop,
Up he goes
To the tree top!

Whirly, twirly,
Round and round,
Down he scampers
To the ground.

Furly, curly,
What a tail!
Tall as a feather,
Broad as a snail!

Where's his supper?
In the shell.
Snap, crack,
Out it fell.

List of rhyming words

hop - top

____

____

____

____

____

Perfect Pairs

Match the male animals to their female partners.

A	B
leopard	mare
cow	hen
lion	goose
peacock	drake
tiger	vixen
rooster	bull
gander	tigress
duck	leopardess
fox	peahen
stallion	lioness

FIND MY FRIENDS

Help the Vocabird find his friends by colouring the path with his female friends pink and his male friends blue. The starting points are given to you.

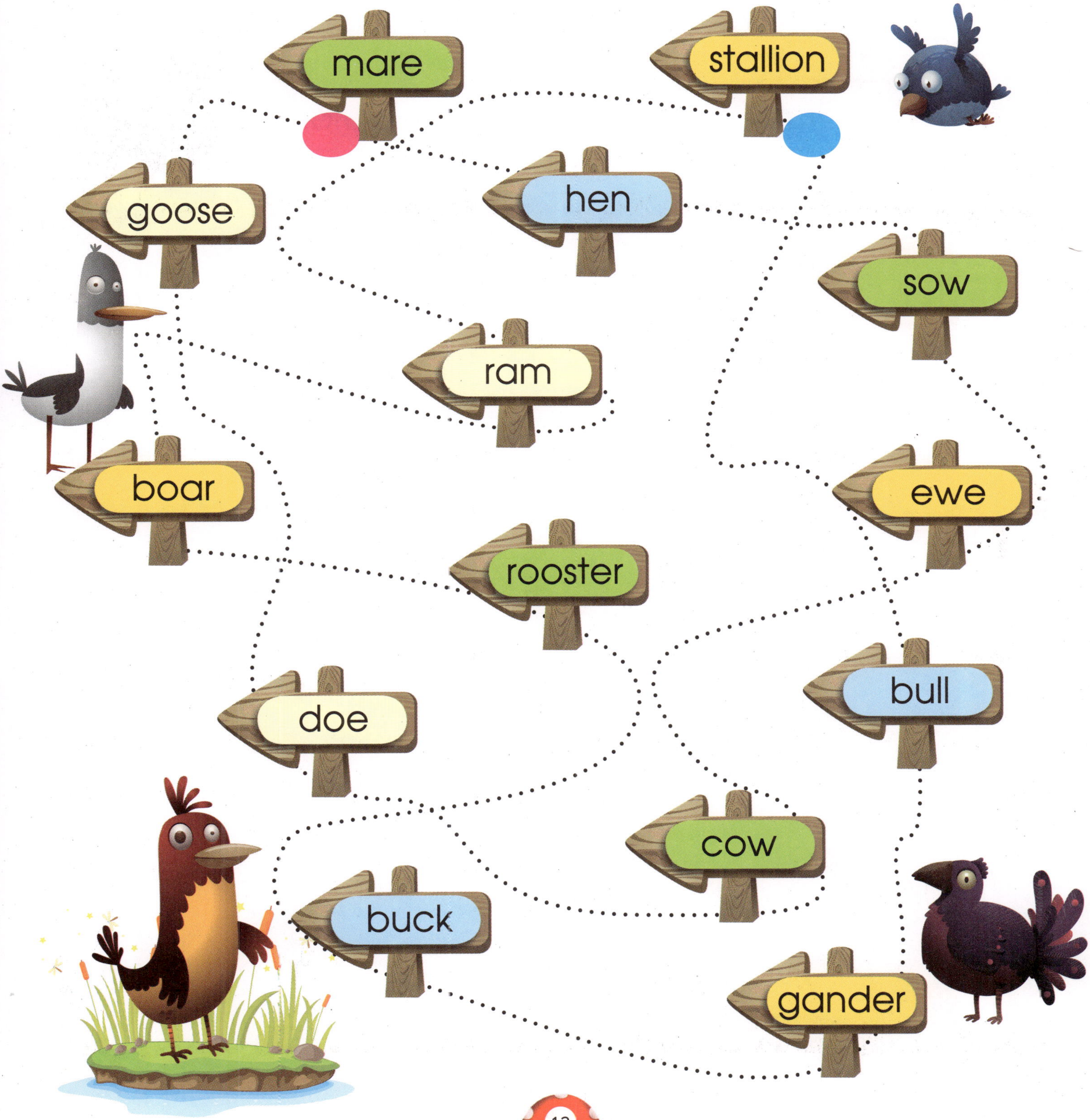

Where's Everyone?

Help the Vocabird to spot and circle different animal habitats in the puzzle given below.

domestic ocean forest desert

farm polar wetland

p	o	l	a	r	a	u	x	k	q
c	o	c	e	a	n	w	y	d	x
f	a	r	m	o	a	j	g	o	l
q	r	p	d	h	e	h	d	m	q
k	v	p	e	i	q	c	z	e	g
w	v	b	s	k	t	h	h	s	a
r	v	o	e	s	s	u	i	t	x
b	f	o	r	e	s	t	o	i	l
y	s	u	t	g	a	q	l	c	z
i	w	e	t	l	a	n	d	s	r

Home Sweet Home

Fill in the blanks to help the Vocabird learn about animals and their habitats.

live in deserts	live in oceans	live on farms
live in extreme cold climates	live in forests	live with people in houses

1) Domestic animals - live with people in houses.

2) Ocean animals - ____________________.

3) Forest animals - ____________________.

4) Desert animals - ____________________.

5) Farm animals - ____________________.

6) Polar animals - ____________________.

Going Home

Match the animals to their habitats.

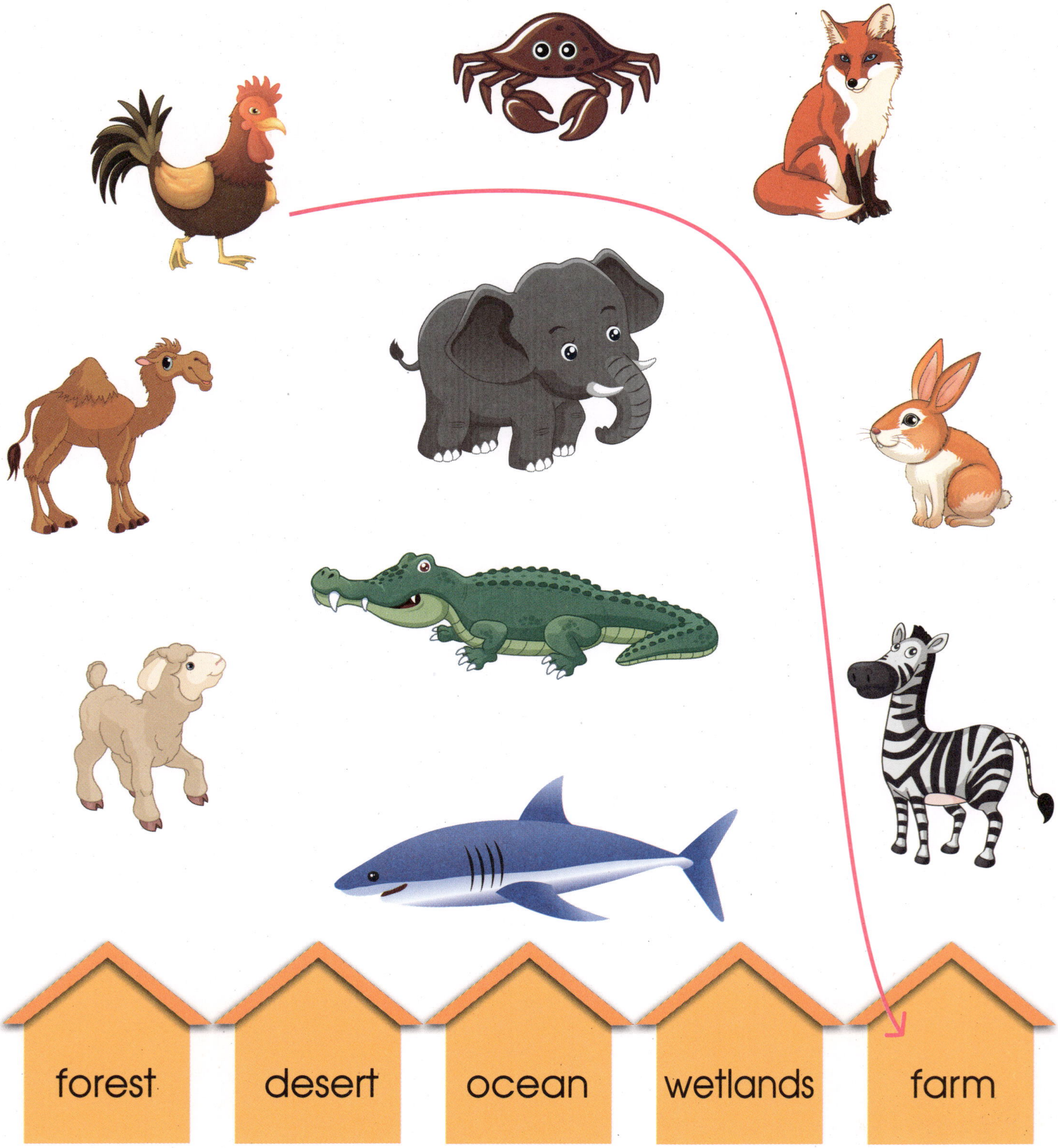

HOMELY MATCH

Match the houses to their names.

hut | building | bungalow

treehouse | tent

Pink or Blue?

Colour the circle below the female gender with a pink crayon and the male gender with a blue crayon.

boy

girl

woman

man

grandmother

grandfather

princess prince

WE ARE FAMILY

Look at the family picture and help the Vocabird fill in the blanks.

Grandfather's name – John

Grandmother's name – __________

Father's name – __________

Mother's name – __________

Sister's name – __________

Brother's name – __________

Baby's name – __________

House Hunting

Fill in the blanks using the words given at the bottom of the page.

1) Places with very little rainfall have flat roof houses.

2) People who travel a lot live in a ________________, which helps them to move around easily.

3) Places with heavy rainfall have ________________.

4) Eskimos live in an ________________.

5) Houses with eight sides are called ________________.

6) The Queen of England lives in a ________________.

7) A ________________ house is made of wood.

8) A house made from natural materials is known as ________________.

palace | caravan | igloo | log

sloping roof houses | octagon houses | kaccha house | flat roof houses

Vehicle Woes

Help the Vocabird identify the vehicles and fill in the blanks with the correct letters.

t r a m

y_ _ _ _

s_ _ _ t_ _

t_ _ c_ _ r

t_ _c_

TRAVEL BUDDIES

Write "land", "water" or "air" under each mode of transport.

Voca tip: Some vehicles travel on land, some vehicles sail in water and some fly in the air.

water

Useful Utilities

Fill in the blanks with the correct option.

1) We fill water in the ___jug___.

home | jug | hand

2) We open the ________ to get fresh air.

basket | pan | window

3) We unlock the door with a ________.

key | apple | toes

4) We use a ________ to cut vegetables.

light | bulb | knife

5) At night, we switch on the ________ to see clearly.

fan | car | tube light

6) People keep a ________ under their head before going to sleep.

fan | pillow | nose

Household Hunt

Circle the household items from the pictures given below.

Match Making

Help the Vocabird connect the words to their synonyms.

start

delight

away

last

tough

right

garbage

hint

gap

begin

tip

rubbish

correct

final

hard

hole

joy

absent

Opposites Attract

Look at the words given below and draw a star below the pair of antonyms for the Vocabird.

day night ★ hot warm

ring sing north south in out

sharp blunt cage lion

stand sit light silly start stop

Collective Choices

Fill in the blanks with collective nouns.

Voca tip: Collective nouns are words which represent a group of things, people, etc.

gaggle	pack	flock	swarm
pride	school	herd	bouquet

1) A <u>flock</u> of birds flew out of his window last night.

2) A ________ of bees attacked Farmer Jones.

3) The shepherd led his ________ of sheep up the mountain.

4) I saw a ________ of fish swimming in the pond.

5) Father gave a ________ of flowers to Mother on her birthday.

6) We saw a ________ of lions when we visited Africa.

7) The endless quacking came from the ________ of geese at the farm.

8) A ________ of wolves howled at the full moon.

Spot 'Em All

This Vocabird is looking for common nouns. Spot and circle them from the words given below.

Voca tip: Common nouns are a common name given to a group of things, animals, etc.

books

team

company

sad

watch

bye

cry

animals

capital

happy

SCRAMBLE HUNT

Unscramble the words in the clue boxes. Spot and circle them in the grid below.

grnee	lalh	rma	bena	etki
sudt	sewt	ckpa	aceg	locud

q	s	g	r	e	e	n	e	w	x
d	u	s	t	r	w	e	s	t	c
x	d	x	o	h	l	m	w	h	l
n	b	e	a	n	j	e	n	a	o
v	t	v	r	t	c	v	o	l	u
b	p	a	c	k	a	p	c	l	d
n	j	w	d	c	g	n	a	k	l
m	k	i	t	e	e	b	r	m	b
l	l	n	f	s	f	s	m	e	s
g	f	g	h	f	z	t	d	i	h

Getting Picky

Sort the words given below in the correct columns.

student | problem | bunch | year

flight | flock | hand | troop

band | system

Collective Nouns
student

Common Nouns
flock

ANSWERS

Page 2

Page 3

Page 5

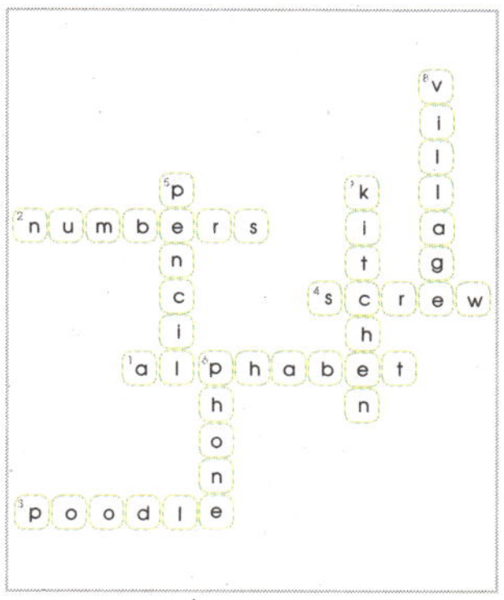

Page 6

Page 7

Page 8

Page 9

Page 10

Page 11

Page 12

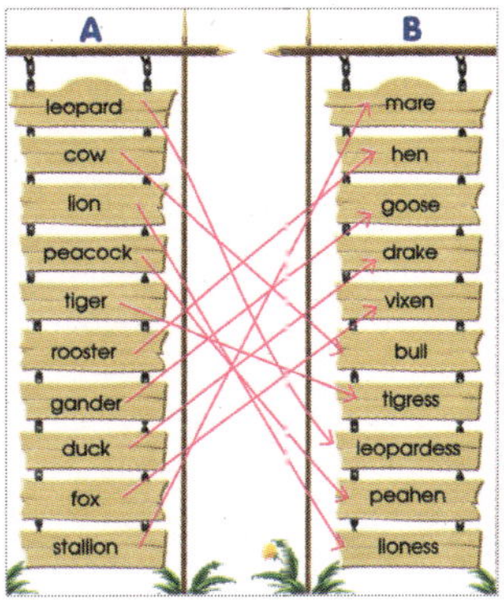

Page 13

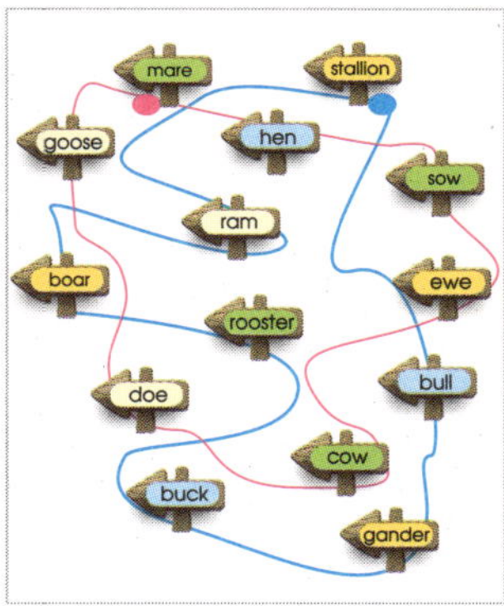

Page 14

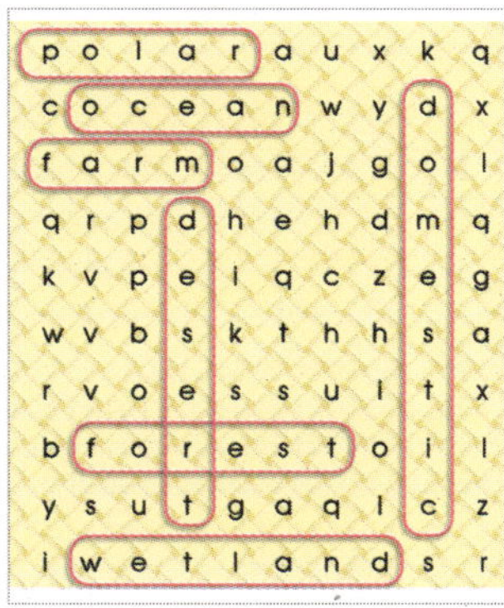

Page 15

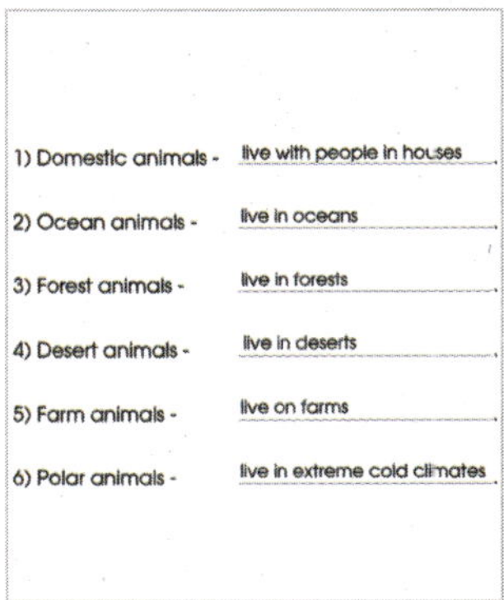

Page 16

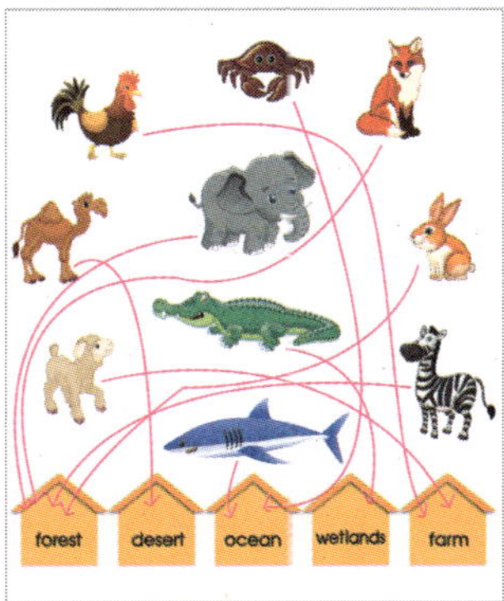

Page 17

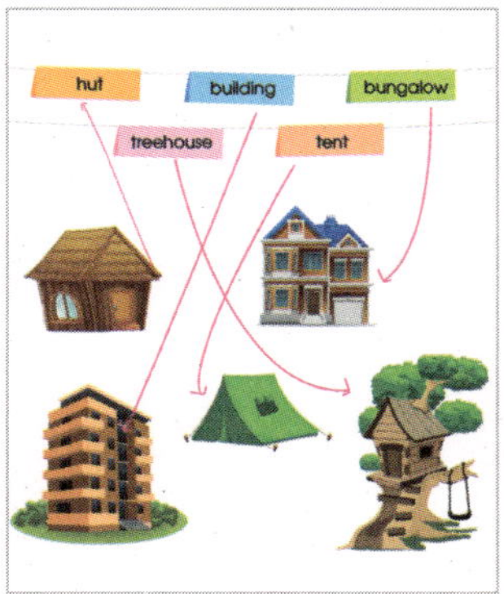

Page 18

ANSWERS

Page 19

Grandfather's name – John
Grandmother's name – Peggy
Father's name – Ron
Mother's name – Myra
Sister's name – Jenny
Brother's name – Ashton
Baby's name – Dan

Page 20

1) Places with very little rainfall have flat roof houses.
2) People who travel a lot live in a caravan, which helps them to move around easily.
3) Places with heavy rainfall have sloping roof houses.
4) Eskimos live in an igloo.
5) Houses with eight sides are called octagon houses.
6) The Queen of England lives in a palace.
7) A log house is made of wood.
8) A house made from natural materials is known as kaccha house.

Page 21

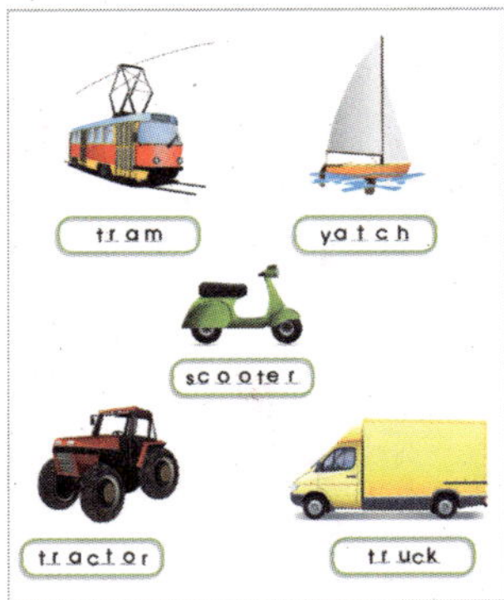

Page 22

Page 23

1) We fill water in the jug.
home jug hand
2) We open the window to get fresh air.
basket pan window
3) We unlock the door with a key.
key apple toes
4) We use a knife to cut vegetables.
light bulb knife
5) At night, we switch on the tube light to see clearly.
fan car tube light
6) People keep a pillow under their head before going to sleep.
fan pillow nose

Page 24

Page 25

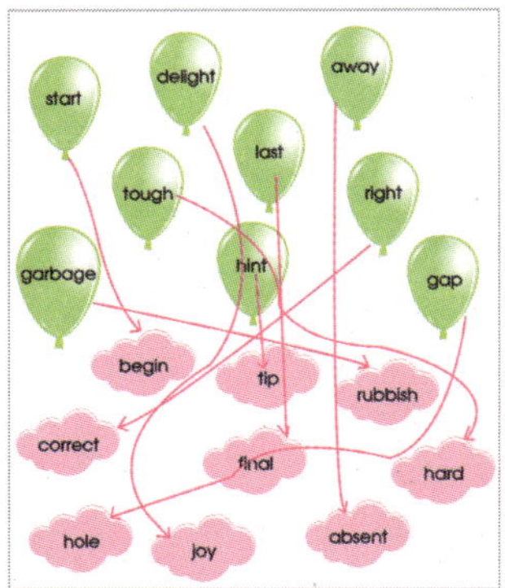

Page 26

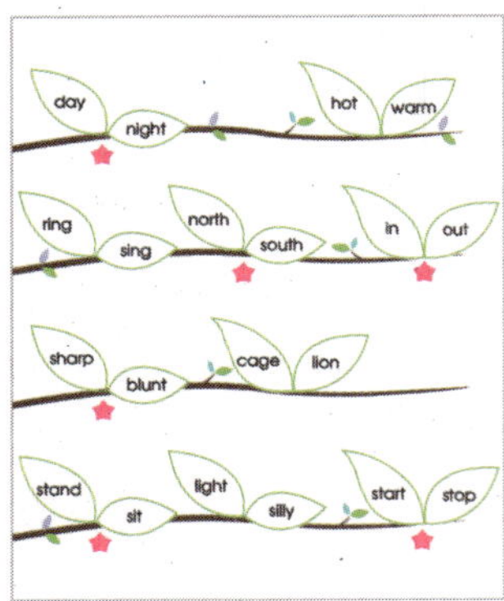

Page 27

1) A flock of birds flew out of his window last night.
2) A swarm of bees attacked Farmer Jones.
3) The shepherd led his herd of sheep up the mountain.
4) I saw a school of fish swimming in the pond.
5) Father gave a bouquet of flowers to Mother on her birthday.
6) We saw a pride of lions when we visited Africa.
7) The endless quacking came from the gaggle of geese at the farm.
8) A pack of wolves howled at the full moon.

Page 28

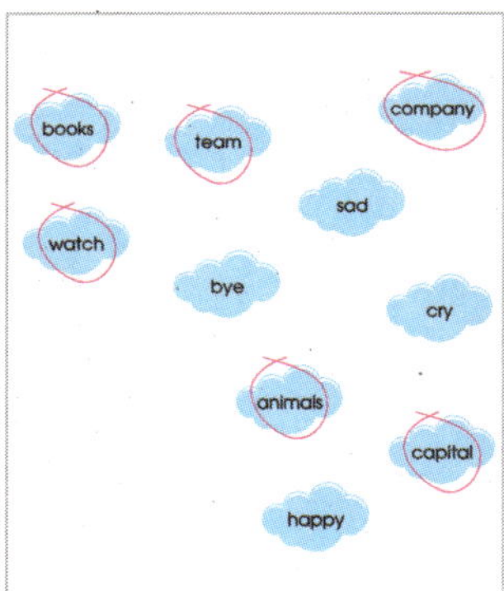

Page 29

q	s	g	r	e	e	n	e	w	x
d	u	s	t	r	w	e	s	t	c
x	d	x	o	h	l	m	w	h	l
n	b	e	a	n	j	e	n	a	o
v	t	v	r	t	c	v	o	l	u
b	p	a	c	k	a	p	c	l	d
n	j	w	d	c	g	n	a	k	l
m	k	i	t	e	e	b	r	m	b
l	l	n	f	s	f	s	m	e	s
g	f	g	h	f	z	t	d	i	h

Page 30

Collective Nouns
student
bunch
flight
troop
band

Common Nouns
flock
problem
year
hand
system